168110

The Life of a
GUINEA PIG

Clare Hibbert

Raintree

Chicago, Illinois

Printed and bound in China by the South China Printing Company

08 07 06 05 04
10 9 8 7 6 5 4 3 2 1

Library of Congress Cataloging-in-Publication Data:

Hibbert, Clare, 1970-
  Life of a guinea pig / Clare Hibbert.
      p. cm. -- (Life cycles)
Summary: A simple introduction to the life cycle of this rodent that is a popular pet all around the world.
Includes bibliographical references
  ISBN 1-4109-0538-1 (hc)
  1. Guinea pigs--Life cycles--Juvenile literature.
[1. Guinea pigs.]
I. Title. II. Series: Life cycles (Chicago, Ill.)
  QL737.R634H53 2004
  599.35'92--dc21

2003006587

Acknowledgments
The publishers would like to thank the following for permission to reproduce photographs: p. 4 Petra Wegner/Foto Natura/FLPA; p. 5 Leo Batten/FLPA; pp. 8, 9, 10, 11, 14, 16, 28 Peter Gurney; pp. 12, 13, 15, 17, 18, 20, 25, 27 Jane Burton/Warren Photographic; p. 19 Minden Pictures; p. 21 T & P Gardner; p. 22 Paul Beard Photo Agency; p. 23 DK Images. p. 24 Foto Natura Stock; p. 26 Frank W. Lane.

Cover photograph of a guinea pig, reproduced with permission of Foto Natura.

The publishers would like to thank Janet Stott for her assistance in the preparation of this book.

Every effort has been made to contact copyright holders of any material reproduced in this book. Any omissions will be rectified in subsequent printings if notice is given to the publishers.

Contents

Any words appearing in the text in bold, **like this,** are explained in the Glossary.

The Guinea Pig

Guinea pigs belong to a family of animals called **mammals.** Dogs, people, and bears are also mammals. All mammals have fur or hair. Baby mammals grow inside their mother and feed from her milk when they are first born.

The guinea pig's closest relatives are rats and mice. Like them, the guinea pig has long front teeth for gnawing at things. Mammals that gnaw like this are called **rodents**.

There are different types of guinea pig. This rough-haired one has fur that goes in all directions.

Growing up

Just as you grow bigger year by year, a guinea pig grows and changes, too. It can live for up to eight years. The different stages of the guinea pig's life make up its **life cycle**.

Where guinea pigs live

Guinea pigs are sometimes called cavies. All over the world, people keep them as pets. Wild cavies live in the rocky mountains and wide grasslands of South America.

Pet guinea pigs, like their wild cousins, enjoy being outside. They nibble the grass and relax in the sunshine.

A Guinea Pig's Life

The **life cycle** of a guinea pig begins when a male and a female guinea pig **mate.** About nine weeks later, the female gives birth to a **litter** of **pups.**

The pups play and explore while they are growing up. By the time they are three months old, they are adults. Soon, they are able to mate and have their own pups.

Long life

Pet guinea pigs can live to be about eight years old. In the wild, a guinea pig usually lives for about three years. A wild guinea pig does not have someone to feed it every day or to keep it safe from other animals.

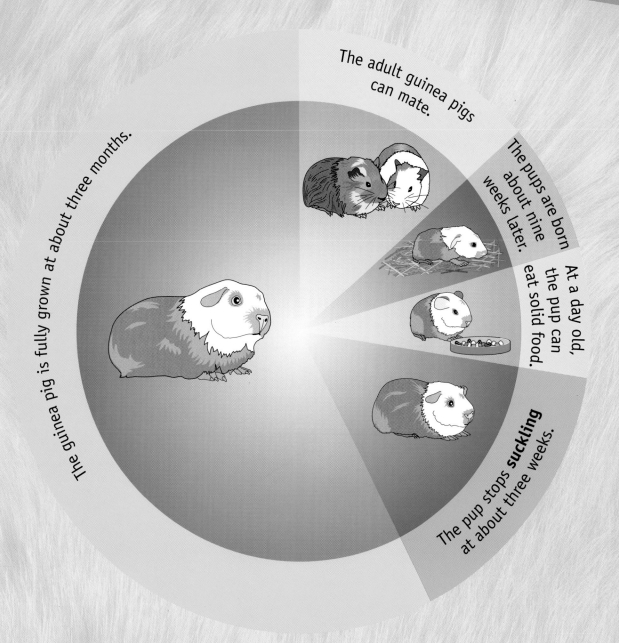

The adult guinea pigs can mate.

The pups are born about nine weeks later.

At a day old, the pup can eat solid food.

The pup stops **suckling** at about three weeks.

The guinea pig is fully grown at about three months.

This diagram shows the life cycle of a guinea pig, from newborn pup to adult.

Arrival

Female guinea pigs are called **sows** and their babies are called **pups.** There are usually two to four pups in a **litter.** Each newborn pup weighs about the same as a large egg.

Cord cutting

When the pup is born, the sow bites the **umbilical cord.** This cord carried food to the pup while it was growing inside her.

The guinea pig pup is born inside a little bag of skin. The mother tears this open with her teeth.

Have you ever seen a newborn mouse? It has no fur and its eyes are shut tight. Guinea pigs are different. They are born furry and their eyes open right away. They even have teeth, which means that they will be able to start eating solid food when they are just a day old.

Fatherly care

Male guinea pigs are called **boars.** They help the female guinea pigs look after the pups. They even purr to the pups. The sound makes the pups feel safe.

This little pup is just a few hours old.

First Hours

Even when a **pup** is just a few minutes old, it is already hungry. It finds its way to its mother's **teat** to drink her milk. This is called **suckling.**

Milk magic

Guinea pig **sows** feed their pups for the first three weeks of life. The pups suckle every half hour or so.

The guinea pig mother sits up to feed her pups.

The milk is full of **nutrients** that help the pups grow. It also contains a special ingredient that helps them fight off illnesses.

Sniffing the air

Guinea pig pups have a good sense of smell from the moment they are born. They soon learn to recognize other members of their family just by their **scent.**

Exploring!

Guinea pig **pups** are very **inquisitive.** Once their bellies are full of milk, they start to explore their surroundings. Some newborn animals cannot walk, but guinea pig pups can even run when they are just three hours old. They often race around the nest, taking in all the new sights and smells.

By twitching their whiskers, the pups sense the world around them. Whiskers even allow guinea pigs to move around in the dark without bumping into things.

Staying close

Although the pups are playful and noisy, they are careful to stick close to their mother. A strange noise is enough to scare them. When they are frightened, they cuddle up to the **sow.** She reassures them with purring noises.

Guinea pig talk

When a sow wants to call her pups, she grunts, and the pups squeak to call her. Purring is a sign of feeling peaceful and happy. Guinea pigs can also squeal, scream, chatter, whine, and whistle.

Taking a Nap

Like all babies, guinea pig **pups** need plenty of sleep in the first few days after they are born. Playing and exploring can be very tiring. Their little bodies are so busy growing that they need a lot of rest.

Pet guinea pigs usually sleep through the night and are up and playing during the day. The pups also take short naps throughout the day. They snuggle up to their mother while they doze. The **sow** needs the sleep, too.

The pups cuddle up to their mother for warmth.

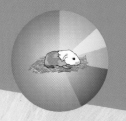

Alarm calls

In the wild, guinea pigs need to be ready to run at the first sign of danger. Although pet guinea pigs are safe from danger, they act the same way. They never go into a deep sleep. Their ears are always busy listening. The sow and her pups wake up at the slightest noise.

On the alert! This wide-eyed pup has just woken up.

Feeding

Wild guinea pigs eat grasses and seeds. They eat only plants as food. The guinea pig **pups** start nibbling plant foods when they are one day old, even though they are still **suckling.**

Pet guinea pig pups eat the same dried food as adults.

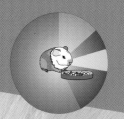

Pig food

Pet guinea pigs always have plenty of hay to eat. Their owners also give them guinea pig food and fresh vegetables. Guinea pig food is usually a mix of seeds, grains, and dried vegetables. Fresh vegetables are very important because they contain **vitamin C.** Like people, guinea pigs must eat foods that contain vitamin C every day.

Growing pups

Guinea pigs grow up at an amazing rate. When it is born, a pup weighs about the same as a large egg. Over its first three weeks of life, the pup more than doubles in weight. No wonder—it spends so much time eating!

Fresh greens are a good source of vitamin C.

Home Turf

Wild guinea pigs live in family groups called **colonies.** Over the first week of life, the young **pups** start to explore their surroundings, but they never stray too far from their mother.

The place where an animal lives is called its **habitat.** Wild guinea pigs live in South America. They make their homes among the rocky peaks and on the grassy plains.

In the wild, guinea pigs find a good hiding spot in rocks.

Hiding places

During the day, guinea pigs stay out of sight of **predators**—animals that hunt other animals for food. They rest in burrows, but they do not dig them for themselves. They find an old burrow that another animal has left behind. Wild guinea pigs also nest in gaps in the rocks or hide in the scrubby grasses.

Big bird

The Andean condor is the largest flying bird in the world. It soars high above the Andes, where some wild guinea pigs live. Most of the time it eats dead meat called carrion. Sometimes, though, it kills and eats living animals such as guinea pigs or even deer.

Dangers

Wild guinea pigs spend about six hours a day feeding. They are busiest at dawn and dusk, when the light is dim and it is harder for **predators** to spot them.

Stampede!

Baby guinea pigs first go outside to feed when they are just hours old, but they stay close to their parents. If any guinea pig senses danger, it gives an alarm call. Then the guinea pigs scatter in all directions. They head for cover with surprising speed.

Wild guinea pigs need to be on the alert in case of predators.

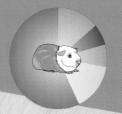

Still as statues

Guinea pigs do not always run from danger. Sometimes they freeze and stay perfectly still instead. This is a good idea. Predators are best at spotting movement. By keeping still, the guinea pig can be almost invisible.

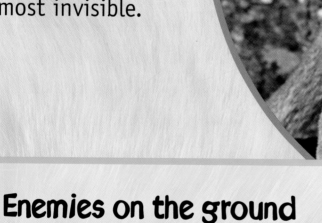

Enemies on the ground

Wild guinea pigs are always on the lookout for danger. A lot of animals would love to catch a plump, juicy guinea pig. There are hungry snakes in the grass, and big cats such as pumas.

Fully Grown

Guinea pigs stop growing when they are three months old. Now they are adults. In the wild, young **boars** often leave home when they become adults. There is no room in the group, or **colony,** for too many males. A boar must challenge his father to a fight, or go off and start a new group somewhere else.

Male guinea pigs sometimes fight. It is not a good idea to keep them together.

A sow's life

The young females may stay with the group. They do not dare fight with the older females. If they do pick a fight, they will soon get a nip on the ear from other females who have been around longer.

Scent marking

Adult guinea pigs spend a lot of time rubbing at things with their cheeks, backs, and bottoms. They leave **scent** markers to show that this is their land, or **territory**. They also rub each other. By swapping smells, they show that they are part of the same colony.

Ready to Mate

When guinea pigs are adults, they can **mate.** This means that a male and a female can come together to have their own **pups.** A pet **sow** usually mates for the first time when she is between four and seven months old.

Flirting

In the wild guinea pig **colony,** there is one male and about five females. The **boar** comes sniffing around each female every day. He does a little dance to show that he wants to mate.

The boar and sow sniff each other, to show that they both want to mate.

Usually each female sends him away by ignoring him. If that does not work, she kicks or snarls.

Sometimes the boar is lucky. If the time is right, the sow lets him mate with her.

Fancy breeds

When pet guinea pigs of the same breed mate, all their pups are the same breed, too. There are many different types of guinea pig. Rexes have hair that stands straight up, while Satins have amazingly soft, silky coats. There is even a Dalmatian guinea pig—white with black spots.

Some breeds, such as this Peruvian, have very long hair.

Expecting a Litter

The female guinea pig is **pregnant** for about nine weeks. That is how long it takes for the baby guinea pigs to grow inside her. While they are inside her the **pups** are called **embryos.**

As the **sow's** stomach swells she begins to need more food. This is because her body is busy feeding the growing embryos. The mother also feels tired a lot of the time. She takes naps as often as she can.

For most of her pregnancy, the sow does not look any different. At the end, though, she looks very fat.

Stay away

In the last few days before she gives birth, the guinea pig sow does not like anyone to come near her. She is now about twice her normal weight. It is tiring for her to move around and she just wants peace and quiet.

This pregnant sow is just four days away from giving birth to her litter of pups. She needs a lot of rest.

New Pups

Even if the female guinea pig has never had **pups** before, she knows just what to do. She gives birth sitting up. It takes between 10 and 30 minutes for all the pups to be born. There are usually two to four pups in the **litter.**

Mother knows best

Just like her mother, the **sow** tears the bag of skin that is around each pup. She grunts so that the pup comes to her **teat** to drink.

This sow has already given birth to two pups. Now the third one of the litter is being born.

Female guinea pigs have only two teats. If they have more than two pups, the babies must take turns at **suckling.**

The new pups soon grow big and strong. With each one, the **life cycle** starts all over again.

Pig pets

Guinea pig pups should stay with their mother until they are about six weeks old. If you are choosing pet guinea pigs, remember that two males will probably fight. Get two sisters, so that they can keep each other company.

Find Out for Yourself

The best way to find out more about the life cycle of a guinea pig is to watch it happen with your own eyes. Perhaps you could raise some guinea pigs at school. Make sure you find a good home for each one.

Books to read

Ganeri, Anita. *A Pet's Life: Guinea Pig*. Chicago: Heinemann Library, 2003.

Head, Honor. *My Pet: Guinea Pig*. Chicago: Raintree, 2000.

Using the Internet

Explore the Internet to find out more about guinea pigs. Websites can change, and if some of the links below no longer work, don't worry. Use a search engine, such as www.yahooligans.com, and type in keywords such as "guinea pig," "cavy," and "life cycle."

Websites

http://www.enchantedlearning.com/subjects/mammals/rodent/printouts.shtml
Click on "guinea pig" to find a page with lots of facts and a picture to print out and color in.

http://ambleweb.digitalbrain.com/web/rodents
Take a look at this school guinea pig project. It includes videos, still pictures, facts, and advice.

Glossary

boar male guinea pig

colony (of guinea pigs) group of five to ten wild guinea pigs that live together. The group is made up of the male leader, adult females, and pups.

embryo baby animal before it has been born or hatched

habitat place where an animal lives

inquisitive eager to learn about the world around you

life cycle all the different stages in the life of a living thing, such as an animal or plant

litter group of baby animals that are all born to the same mother at the same time

mammal animal that has fur or hair, and that gives birth to its young, and feeds them on milk. People are mammals, and so are guinea pigs, cats, and dogs.

mate when a male and female animal come together to make eggs or babies.

nutrients substances found in food that help an animal to grow

predator animal that hunts other animals and eats them for food

pregnant when a female has a baby growing inside her body

pup baby guinea pig

rodent small mammal that has long front teeth for gnawing. These front teeth never stop growing. Guinea pigs, mice, and rats are all rodents.

scent smell

sow female guinea pig

suckling drinking mother's milk

teat mother animal's nipple, where her babies drink milk from

territory area of land where an animal or group of animals lives. Animals often mark their territory by leaving their scent on rocks and tree trunks, warning other animals to stay away.

umbilical cord tube that links a baby mammal to its mother while it is growing inside her. The cord carries food and air to the baby.

vitamin C substance found in some fruits and vegetables that the body needs to be healthy

Index